Let's Talk About Autism
In Early Childhood

Let's Talk About
Autism
In Early Childhood

KAREN GRIFFIN ROBERTS

Fourth Lloyd Productions, LLC
Burgess, VA

For permissions write to:
Fourth Lloyd Productions, LLC
512 Old Glebe Point Road
Burgess, VA 22432
email: stodart@kaballero.com
www.FourthLloydProductions.com

ISBN: 978-0-9889391-3-4
Library of Congress Control Number: 2014945827
Printed in the United States of America

TABLE OF CONTENTS

Table of Contents *(cont'd)*

Acknowledgments

This book is written for and dedicated to the many families with whom I share the autism journey—both inside and outside of the classroom. I thank you for your continued support as we strive to foster successful social and educational experiences for all of our children.

I am grateful to everyone who helped to advance this project. To Ana Hoover, who helped me gather information from families to learn the many questions each has about autism, and for lending to me her expertise. A special thanks to Nadine Bolkhovitinov, Kristen Scott, Judy Polivy, Margaret Stout, Cindy Shupe and Robin Weisman who graciously read through the entire document and provided reviews, advisements and encouragements. Thank you Mary Fannin—once again—for copy editing and finding and fixing grammar and typos.

I am especially grateful to Sarah Pavitt and Heidi Graff for providing me with their autism expertise to edit this book for technical correctness. Thank you for your patience and guidance on the ever-changing information in autism diagnosis and treatments.

I am always grateful for the artwork, design and publishing advice received from Richard and Nancy Stodart of Fourth Lloyd Productions. They continue to provide authors the inspiration and professionalism necessary to bring shared questions and answers to our special education families.

Finally, to little learners and their families who inspire me daily: Thank you for all of the gifts you share.

MY AUTISM

I have autism.
I have two sides,
And things are sometimes cloudy.
But, I'm like a little seed that
Grows into a flower.
I have courage,
And I am supported by family, faith and friends
Who make me feel the warmth
In my heart.

– Kevin David Roberts –

In her book, *Let's Talk About Autism in Early Childhood*, Karen Griffin Roberts demystifies the world of autism in easy-to-understand language that parents, grandparents and anyone who cares about a young person with autism will find illuminating. Not only does Roberts include the most current information from the DSM-5 diagnosis of autism, translated into understandable language, but she also ties this new definition to young people, their struggles, and the questions that their challenges raise for those who love them.

There is a reason the symbol for the autism movement is a bunch of colorful puzzle pieces linked together. There are many aspects of autism that puzzle parents and educators alike. Sometimes, when I'm teaching and watching a child, who cannot navigate a social interaction with another, settle in at the puzzle table trying to solve the most complicated picture with no one helping her, I wonder at the magnificence of the human brain. I wonder that so much variety is manifested, and yet the simplest human interaction of requesting from another might require the support of assistive technology, another adult modeling the verbalization, and many repetitions. Roberts makes the variety of the faces of autism look like our little friends in preschool, trying to navigate their way through a world that is difficult to comprehend.

Here in this resource, the readers will find clear and simple explanations for questions that naturally crop up with young children with autism, answers to questions that have been thought, "Googled" and still not answered, and ideas for educational programming that bring the human side to each educational decision. These are not autistic children to be shunned, but children with autism to be understood and embraced for who they are, and to be educated with rigorous expectation for strong positive outcomes of communication and social interaction.

Playing games, singing, listening to music and reading to your child are three of the suggestions Roberts puts forward for encouraging the language development of young children with autism. She outlines the ways that social narratives can help young children grow socially. She describes the bombardment of stimuli that a young child with autism faces every day coupled with the inability to describe her pain to another. Ideas for teaching the difficult concept of another's mind, the "theory of mind," and teaching joint attention, or that capability of seeing things through another's eyes, are put forward in a very gentle and understandable way. Roberts also tackles the tricky terrain of sensory processing disorder with some key definitions and facts to make the diagnosis comprehensible. Guidance shared among all the team working with a child is presented in a thoughtful way that takes care to incorporate the observations of everyone involved with the individual child's development and academic success.

Roberts speaks with the authority of someone who has lived the intense daily challenges and finally the rewarding journey of caring deeply with all her heart for her son, now a young man who can tell us all how it was to be a young child with autism. The very kind and insightful approach Roberts promotes for establishing social communication, for keeping very high expectations for children who do have strengths to offer, for encouraging the persistent efforts and rigorous education through pictures, through modeling, through repetition, and through trying something new, is like a raft in the rough sea for those who are struggling with a new diagnosis of one they love and for those who seek clarity in their journey.

Nadine A Bolkhovitinov, NBCT, Ph.D.
Early Childhood through Young Adulthood
Exceptional Needs Specialist

INTRODUCTION

Let's Talk About Autism in Early Childhood is organized around actual questions that early childhood special education teachers have heard from their autism students' parents. As a special educator and the parent of a son with autism, I am intimately familiar with the concerns and questions that are raised when parents first learn of their child's autism diagnosis.

While it may seem as though in the past ten years autism is a new diagnosis, it is not; it was first studied in the 1940's. For years—both before and after that time—it was misunderstood. Today, with all of the immediate access to information through social media and the Internet, and with current research in neurology, it has become increasingly difficult to keep up with the changes in autism diagnoses, research and discoveries. Autism is now referred to as a major health and educational concern in the United States. Recent statistics indicate one in every 68 children has autism, and prevalence statistics have steadily climbed upward, especially in the past ten years (CDC, 2014). Autism is not only the fastest growing disability category, but it is also more prevalent in children than pediatric cancer, diabetes, and AIDS combined.

This book shares some similarities with the text in my earlier publication, *Embracing Autism in Preschool: Successful Strategies for General Education Teachers* (Fourth Lloyd Productions, 2010). However, *Embracing Autism* was written as a guide to general education teachers to provide strategies for including preschool children with autism in their classrooms. After its publication, I heard from many families who had read the earlier book but who wanted to learn about more areas specific to autism outside of the classroom environment. Thus, *Let's Talk About Autism in Early Childhood* is written in question and answer format for those families who continue to have questions, and for those just beginning to learn about autism. This text is the second in a series following Ana Gamarra Hoover's and my publication of *Let's Talk About Early Language Development* (Fourth Lloyd Productions, 2013).

I cannot possibly fully address all aspects of autism spectrum disorder in this book. And, while my own son is now an adult with autism—and autism is a life-long disorder—as an early childhood special educator, I am more confident in my understanding of autism in early childhood than I am of autism into adulthood. As a very brief introduction of autism in early childhood, this book is intended to help families of young children better understand their child's autism diagnosis and to encourage families to continue to ask questions about autism. Furthermore, as an introduction, I invite you to review the recommended reading resources at the end of this book which provide more detailed information on autism in early childhood.

Chapter ONE

What Is Autism?

My child just received a diagnosis of autism. I have many questions, the first of which is: "What does it mean to have autism?"

Autism is a developmental disorder which affects a person's ability to communicate and interact with others. While autism typically appears during the first three years of life, it may have taken some time before you learned your child does indeed have autism. This is because autism is difficult to diagnose. No two people with an autism diagnosis share the same experiences, interests, successes, ability levels, or challenges.

The American Psychiatric Association (APA) is responsible for guiding professionals who diagnose brain disorders. They publish their standards in *The Diagnostic and Statistical Manual of Mental Disorders,* more commonly referred to as the "DSM." According to the latest DSM-5 (APA, 2013), in order to receive a **diagnosis for autism spectrum disorder**, a person must have:

A. Deficits in social communication and social interaction.

B. Restricted, repetitive patterns of behavior, interests, or activities in at least two of four areas:

    a. Stereotypical or repetitive movements;

    b. Insistence on sameness;

    c. Highly restricted and/or fixative interests;

    d. Have either hypo- or hyper-sensory sensitivity, or unusual interests *in the sensory aspects of his environment.*

C. Symptoms present in the early developmental period (even though the person may not show signs until he is older and struggling socially and/or has had time to learn strategies as he gets older to compensate for autism deficits).

D. Symptoms that cause significant impairment in the person's social life, in his occupation, or other important areas of his education and life.

E. Impairments are not explained by intellectual disability (ID) or a global developmental delay. However, autism can occur with ID, so to distinguish between the two, social communication must fall below what would be expected for the child's general developmental level.

Does my child have to have all of these characteristics to get a diagnosis of autism?

No and yes! This is the APA guideline. This is what developmental physicians will use to learn if your child has autism. However, keep in mind that when your child is being assessed, the professional has a limited amount of time to spend with him and therefore may not see some of the criteria right away. And, you may not see all of these traits in your younger child—especially a very young child who is still in the developmental stage of learning appropriate social skills and social communication (which will be discussed further in this text). Some of the traits may occur in different circumstances or environments and less often, so they are not as apparent. And, of course, Part B of the diagnosis includes four criteria, but only two of the four need to be present to diagnose autism.

What is the difference between autism and autism spectrum disorder?

We often refer to people with autism as "being on the autism spectrum". Because autism affects each individual differently and because there are a wide range of abilities among those with autism, the term "autism spectrum disorder" (or ASD) is used in general conversation when the ability level of the person with autism is either not yet known or is not being specifically addressed.

My son's special education teacher says that in the new DSM, autism is diagnosed by "levels of severity". What does that mean?

That's right.   In the DSM-5 (APA, 2013), the American Psychiatric Association has outlined levels of autism according to severity. Levels of autism range from "requires support" to "requires very substantial support", as indicated below:

Autism, Level 1: Requires support: "Without supports in place, deficits in social communication cause noticeable impairments"...

Autism, Level 2:   Requires substantial support: "Marked deficits in verbal and nonverbal social communication skills; social impairments apparent even with supports in place; limited initiation of social interactions; and reduced or abnormal responses to social overtures from others"...

Autism, Level 3: Requires very substantial support: "Severe deficits in verbal and nonverbal social communication skills cause severe impairments in functioning, very limited initiation of social interactions, and minimal response to social overtures from others" (p. 30).

I was surprised when my son received his autism diagnosis, because I know other children with autism, and my son is able to do so much more. My developmental physician said he has higher functioning autism—most likely "Asperger's Syndrome". Is Asperger's Syndrome another name for autism?

The American Psychological Association works hard to keep the DSM manual up to date. The earlier DSM-4 outlined autism as a spectrum of different disorders, including: (1) Autistic Disorder; (2) Asperger's Syndrome; (3) Childhood Disintegrative Disorder (CDD); (4) Rett's Disorder; and (5) Pervasive Development Disorder-Not Otherwise Specified (PDD-NOS). Within each one of the autism disorders, there was a separate level of ability. Professionals had to research each disorder to see where a child's diagnosis would fit best. Consideration was given to the child's: IQ; level of social communication; and his level of cooperation with others—or his tendency toward problem behaviors. Professionals also had to consider if the child's autism was accompanied by an intellectual disability or any other mental disorder. You can imagine how difficult it was to consider all of the criteria to diagnose autism.

When the DSM was updated and the DSM-5 was published in 2013, those specific disorder labels were removed. The American Psychiatric Association felt that the five diagnoses were too difficult to separate and that a diagnosis of autism should be labeled by levels of severity.

To answer your question: I'm guessing that if the physician said Aspergers, your son fits the criteria of Autism, Level 1. As I understand Aspergers, I would guess that your son is quite independent. However, if he does not have the supports he needs in place, he probably has a difficult time with social communication, reading social cues and making friends. He may be very articulate, quite bright, but very literal. I expect if he has Aspergers, he does exactly what you tell him to do—nothing more, nothing less—and he may have some significant sensory issues. These are the criteria most associated with the previous diagnosis of Asperger's Syndrome.

There were many debates when the APA first considered establishing new guidelines for an autism diagnosis. Many professionals agreed that Retts, CDD and PDD-NOS should be removed from the criteria, but many more people did *not agree* that Asperger's should be removed from the DSM. This is largely because so many people were beginning to understand Aspergers and the abilities children possess with that particular level of autism.

Yet even with the removal of Asperger's Syndrome from the DSM, there remains a large community of individuals who have come together in the past years who were diagnosed with Asperger's Syndrome. There are also many organizations which support families of people who have received an Asperger's Syndrome diagnosis. I believe, even though it is no longer part of the DSM, that all of the supports in place will continue.

So, are you saying that people diagnosed with Asperger's Syndrome have higher functioning autism?

When describing children with autism, it is common for professionals to use the terms "high" functioning or "low" functioning autism. Lower functioning often implies that the child with autism also has an intellectual disability. Despite the fact that these descriptors are used regularly, they are too limiting—and perhaps offensive. Given the information drafted in the DSM-5, autism level 1-3 is not only a kinder, but a better descriptor of area of need, and a politically correct description of each person's ability. Your developmental physician is the best person to help you learn your child's autism level.

What did I do to cause my son's autism?

You did not cause your son's autism. There are many theories and debates surrounding causation of autism, not all of which are scientifically proven. Research is ongoing, and it is not at all unusual to hear of breakthroughs and theories surrounding autism research. At this time, some of the most common theories are those based on neurological, biological, genetic, environmental factors and childhood vaccines. Let's take a brief look at some of these theories on the following chart.

THEORIES FOR CAUSATION OF AUTISM			
Complied from sources: National Institutes of Health (2010); Autism Society of America, 2014; CDC 2014			
THEORY	EVIDENCE-BASED CAUSE	POSSIBLE CAUSE More time and testing are needed to determine if this is a cause for ASD	NOT A CAUSE Current Research does not support this theory
Neurological	—abnormal volume (size) in areas of the brain —overactive "thinning" of neurons (over pruning) —lack of, or abundance of neurotransmitters for neurons relaying information —abnormality in neurotransmitters which alter the central nervous system —25% of people with autism also have seizures which can cause brain damage		

THEORY	EVIDENCE-BASED CAUSE	POSSIBLE CAUSE More time and testing are needed to determine if this is a cause for ASD	NOT A CAUSE Current Research does not support this theory
Genetic	—age of both parents over 40 years: first-born offspring more likely to have autism —chromosome abnormality —inverted duplication of a portion of chromosome 15 —low birth weight in girls (no findings in theory for low birth weight for boys) —higher levels of testosterone which is apparent in ADHD and autism—both more prevalent in males—could be a genetic risk		
Biological		—impaired immune system resulting in inflammation and susceptibility to infection which causes pain and thus behavior problems for those who cannot communicate pain —poor diet, metabolic vulnerabilities/ disorders and their resulting tissue damage produce nutritional deficiencies which can impair brain processes;	

THEORY	EVIDENCE-BASED CAUSE	POSSIBLE CAUSE More time and testing are needed to determine if this is a cause for ASD	NOT A CAUSE Current Research does not support this theory
Biological (cont'd)		food or food additives and/or allergies; problems with digestion (i.e., food not being digested completely and/or reflux); leaky gut" —tiny holes in intestinal tract caused by an overgrowth of yeast which cause medical problems and pain which may contribute to behavior problems	
Environmental		—vulnerable metabolic system function impaired by exposure to chemicals —infections and other agents —environmental exposures impair development and function of the brain and intelligence —the result of an increasing unhealthy environment	
Childhood Vaccines			—vaccines for seasonal influenza, Diphtheria-Tetanus-Pertussis (DPT), Diphtheria-Tetanus-Pertussis (DTaP), and Hepatitis B contain thimerosal (mercury) —Measles, Mumps & Rubella (MMR)

THEORY	EVIDENCE-BASED CAUSE	POSSIBLE CAUSE	NOT A CAUSE
Childhood Vaccines (cont'd)			—individual immunizations, or stress on the body from combined sets of immunizations

It is a bit daunting, isn't it? This is only a handful of theories available for consideration. It is important to remind yourself that there is no "quick fix" or cure. While many of these theories have been investigated, neurological and genetic have the most research behind them to support these categories as evidence-based causations. I'd like to give you a word of advice: While I understand it is all very puzzling, I hope you will try not to focus on what might have been but instead, move forward in the direction of all of the opportunities available to your child.

I'd heard a lot about autism before my daughter was diagnosed, but I am feeling quite alone at this time because I don't know anyone right now who is on my same journey. Everyone who learns she has autism tells me what I should be doing to help her. Is this unusual?

I understand, and this is not at all unusual. You have no doubt come across people who don't understand, but are still willing—hopefully with your best interests in mind—to give you their advice on "what they've heard" about cures and therapies. Believe me, this will be the norm. Always be mindful that you know your daughter better than anyone. You know what is best for her and your family. This is true of children with or without autism.

Receiving a diagnosis can be frightening. However, you may soon realize the benefit of an autism label when your daughter becomes qualified for services to help her educationally and socially. And, believe me—you are not at all alone in this journey. As indicated in the Introduction of this book, the Centers for Disease Control (CDC, 2014) reports that one in every 68 children is diagnosed with autism. While autism is not particularly prevalent among any racial, ethnic or educational level, it is five times more prevalent in boys than in girls (one in 42 boys; one in 189 girls). These numbers include only those children up to eight years old who have received a solid diagnosis of autism. There are many young children yet to be diagnosed.

Now that your daughter is diagnosed, I hope you can take comfort in knowing that you will quickly become part of a community of families all eager to learn as much as they can about autism. I am including several resources and support networks at the end of this book which I hope will not only provide you with more support, but will also provide you with more information on autism spectrum disorder.

My developmental physician says my son has autism and an attention deficit disorder. Do all children with autism have an attention deficit disorder?

Not all children with autism have an attention deficit disorder. However, autism is very often accompanied by other mental health or developmental disabilities (Kutscher, 2005). Children with autism might have any one, or a combination of disorders, including, but not limited to: attention deficit disorder; a specific learning disability; sensory processing disorder; an intellectual disability; obsessive compulsive disorder; Tourette's syndrome; or bipolar disorder. You may hear professionals refer to the combination of mental and health diagnoses as "comorbidities".

Should I tell my son he has autism? If so, when should I tell him?

That is a very personal and individual decision. You are the only person who can make the decision to tell your son or when to tell your son. If you do choose to have this discussion, you might begin as you discuss different ways of learning and/or different traits among his peers. For instance, a dialog could begin when you are discussing his peers, as in, "Ian sure is good at soccer, and you are a great swimmer" or " Jason has many friends. You like playing with Jason, but sometimes you need help making more friends."

If your son is diagnosed with level one autism and needs help understanding obvious differences in learning styles or help in advocating for himself, this conversation might be especially helpful for him. Your son might actually be relieved to understand that the reason it is so difficult for him to join in play with peers is because he has autism.

I'm a bit overwhelmed right now. Can you explain further the traits which must be present to give a child a diagnosis of autism? I have not spoken with his pediatrician, but I think my son may have autism.

It can be very overwhelming, and I congratulate you on taking the necessary steps to learn about autism. I encourage you to discuss your concerns with your child's developmental physician. In the meantime, let me help you to better understand by taking a look—in the following chapters.

CHAPTER TWO

Autism Diagnosis DSM-5
Part A: Deficits In Social Communication

Social Communication

What does it mean to have deficits in social communication?

Language and communication represent a natural process. To engage in social communication, there must be a desire to communicate with others. During the preschool years (ages two to five), young children often do not have the vocabulary nor do they always understand how to appropriately share or express feelings. As each year passes, they acquire new vocabulary, their sentence lengths increase and they begin to use language logically and imaginatively. By age five, children have acquired most of the sentence structure of their language. They are able to communicate with peers and adults, make requests, make comments and choose appropriate speech based on the current topic of conversation (Hoover & Roberts, 2013).

However, language and communication present significant challenges to children with autism. The range of ability can vary from non-verbal to verbal competency. It is believed, however, that in autism the one impairment that appears to impact all children is pragmatic language or the social use of language.

What is "pragmatic language"?

Pragmatic language includes the use of body language, gestures, appropriate social communication, the intent of the communication and the amount of information given to a listener. Pragmatic language also includes varying your communication to properly address the person to whom you are speaking (Hoover & Roberts, 2013). For instance, I would talk to your child in the classroom differently than I would speak to you at a parent-teacher conference.

Pragmatic language begins as an infant when your child first gazes into your eyes. He then begins to babble. You might reply with a babble—and your infant replies in turn as if you are carrying on a conversation.

Later, your toddler is taking turns in conversation by stringing sounds together with correct intonations used for questions and comments. This is called jargon. He might also begin pointing and calling your attention to things. This pointing and sharing interest with another person is an important part of social communication that we call "joint attention" (Hoover & Roberts, 2013).

My son answers yes and no questions, but he sort of goes off on his own when people are sitting around talking. Is this what it means to have problems with pragmatic language?

That is a piece of it, yes. As I mentioned earlier, for social communication to be effective there must be a desire to communicate with another person. Children with autism do not always understand another person's feelings or intents in conversation, so they have no incentive to participate in shared communication. They sometimes have solitary interests and talk only about their interests. Children with autism may not use communicative gestures—like pointing or eye gaze—to share information and initiate joint attention.

This is an area I don't understand. My son talks a lot. He recites the alphabet and sings songs when he is playing. So, I know he is speaking. His teacher told me his speech is "non-functional". What does that mean?

This is a common trait in children with autism and a question we hear often as special educators. If your son is not speaking to communicate with you, then he is not using social language. Children with autism often use language which does not relate to the topic of conversation or current situation (Willis, 2006). This is what your son's teacher means by "non-functional communication". His words and his singing serve no purpose in sharing information for a communicative exchange or to share attention to a topic. He has possibly memorized phrases and songs and repeats them from memory rather than using words to communicate.

My son's teacher says his speech is "echolalic". What does that mean?

Echolalic speech is also very common in autism and is another type of non-functional communication. Echolalia occurs when a child with autism repeats—or echoes—what he has heard, rather than answers or comments on your question. For instance, when you ask your child, "May I tie your shoe?" he might echo your phrase saying, "Tie your shoe? Tie your shoe?" rather than answer "Yes" or "No". There is also something called "delayed echolalia", in which a person repeats something he's heard at some other time. Sometimes echolalia is used in a semi-functional way, such as when a child says "Do you want a cookie?" to his parent when he is trying to ask for a cookie. Instead of generating his own question, he repeats his parent's question, "Do you want a cookie?" because in the past, he received a cookie after he was asked that same question.

Copying what others say is actually part of early speech development. When toddlers learn to speak, they often repeat what they've heard and eventually begin to expand on words and phrases to communicate. It is thought that children with autism who use a lot of echolalia might be stuck in that developmental phase of language. However, once they are able to overcome the repeating echolalia, they are better able to learn to communicate more purposefully (Bright Tots, 2014).

Sometimes my son will answer yes or no, but I don't always know if he really understands my question. How can I know if he understands me?

Most children with autism perceive the world in a way that is very concrete and literal. If you ask them a yes or no question, they may answer it and be done with their perception of a conversation. For instance, if you ask, "Did you put your snack in your backpack?" he might reply, "No." It would not occur to him that—if he has not done so—you want him to get his snack and put it in his backpack. You would need to also give him that direction. This is because some children with autism have a difficult time processing information well enough or quickly enough to follow more than one direction at a time.

To answer your question: I do believe your child understands your questions. First, it may take him more time to process your question. Further, because of his inability to understand gestures, others' feelings or intents, and abstract language, he may present deficits in the give and take of social communication. Remember that children with autism often have a difficult time initiating conversation unless they have something that highly motivates them. They rarely communicate or initiate conversation to intentionally socialize. As you learn your child's non-verbal behaviors, help him expand on his wants and needs with visual support. For instance, when he is ready to go outside, ask him if he wants to go to the pool or to the playground and point in the direction for each. Or, show him pictures of the park or pool. This way, you know he understands and will likely use the same strategies.

My son said many words when he was a toddler. He called me "Mama" and his father, "Dada". He is four years old now and doesn't talk at all. What happened to his speech? Will he begin talking again?

As a special educator, this is a question I often hear from families of children who are not speaking. It is a common developmental trait in the history of children on the autism spectrum to speak until they are around two years old and then to stop speaking (Hoover & Roberts, 2013). There are also children on the autism spectrum who have never spoken and others who speak, but their communication is non-functional (as outlined earlier).

You may hear professionals say that your son is "nonverbal" and some in the autism community will say that your son is "voiceless". I wish I had the answer to your question. Your child's developmental physicians and his medical team better understand your child's development and would be the best professionals to ask questions about his verbal ability.

What if he never talks? How will he communicate?

Remember that communication is not all verbal communication. In the special education classroom we use a combination of strategies to help children communicate, including: very basic sign language, picture communication cards, a significant amount of prompting for information, simple gestures, repeated verbal and visual prompts and some assistive technology (Hoover & Roberts, 2013). Individual children respond to particular strategies. As special educators, we hope we can educate the child's family on strategies that are working and expand on them to provide each child many opportunities to communicate.

What can I do to help my child develop appropriate social communication?

This might seem like a daunting task, but I believe one of the best ways for your child to learn social communication is to expose him to every opportunity to be social with same-age peers. Preschool classrooms (general education and special education) all focus on social-emotional development for young children in the classroom. Most of the following strategies I am outlining here are important pieces of any preschool curriculum.

There are so many ways to help your child develop social communication. Strategies can be used for children with limited verbal language, or for those who are totally verbal. Just keep in mind that for appropriate social communication to take place, your child has to learn to understand another person's feelings or intents in conversation, so he has an incentive to participate in shared communication.

Your child may have solitary interests and want to talk only about those interests, so we need to find a way to bring him into conversation by helping him learn to use communicative gestures—like pointing or eye gaze—to initiate joint attention and to share his interests. You'll notice I said "we". You will always be part of a team in your child's education, and you should always depend on your child's professionals to help guide you when you need our support.

First and foremost: even if your child is nonverbal, you should EXPECT that your child will learn to communicate. Just as you expect your child to walk, to run, to climb, to eat on his own, etc., you should expect that your child will communicate. When your child comes to you for something and you know what he wants, wait for him to let you know what he wants. Keep things a bit out of reach so your child has to communicate what he wants. For instance, if you know he wants crackers, say to him, "You want crackers?" and point to them. Take his hand in yours and help him learn to point as you say, "Crackers?" Always give him time to respond in one way or the other. Talk to your child constantly, about your day, what you are doing in the moment, what you are eating, etc. Remember that he can hear; he just needs to hear, see and practice ways to learn to respond. Non-verbal gestures—such as pointing, reaching and nodding—should be used frequently to prompt your child and provide him opportunities to respond (Hoover & Roberts, 2013).

Ask your child's special educator for information and resources. Talk to your child's special educator and ask her what success she has had in the classroom and follow her lead at home. For instance, if your child is learning and using sign language in the classroom, learn and use some basic sign language and use gestures when you are communicating with your child. If your child is using some form of electronic device to communicate, ask his teacher how you can help develop that skill at home (Hoover & Roberts, 2013).

Try communicating with objects and pictures. Some children have success with objects and picture cues. Objects can be used for your child to show you what he wants or to show him what you want him to do. For instance, if you take your child his back pack, he knows it is time for school. Picture cues can be used for visual schedules, places to go, people to know, and for food and other choices offered to your child during the day. For instance, when it is time to get his jacket on to go to the library, you could show your child a picture of his jacket and the library. Even though you verbalize these things, the picture cues help your child organize his thoughts.

Digital pictures of people, places and things work well. Many children enjoy taking the pictures themselves. As a family project, you can help your child organize pictures into schedules and other ideas to communicate. Pictures attract and hold children's attention. They enable children to focus on the message and help reduce anxiety; they make abstract things more concrete and help children express their thoughts (Rao & Gagie, 2006).

You may hear professionals talk about a formal picture communication program called "Picture Exchange Communication System"—referred to as PECS. This program is used in many classrooms for children to exchange cards in conversation (PECS, Pyramid Education, 2008). The program may be at first a bit difficult for a very young child, but, if your child responds well and is progressing with the cards, exchanging a card for one word and then adding phrases and sentences for conversational intent would be a goal.

Play games. Playing games engages children by involving them in taking turns, by encouraging them to communicate to request a turn, and by finding ways to indicate to each other when it is someone else's turn. Play games that require children to interact, such as rolling a ball back and forth to one another. If you have access to a playground with a see-saw, you probably know that it's easier to make the see-saw work if there is a person sharing on the other side!

Use music. Music motivates young children. While he may or may not respond to his name, your child might immediately respond to a familiar tune or something else which highly motivates him. Use familiar tunes. Put words to the tunes when you want your child's attention. Use those familiar tunes along with song-gesture routines to encourage your child to imitate gestures. Pause to provide your child the opportunity to fill in words to tunes.

Read to your child. Reading aloud to your child helps him learn and build vocabulary and helps him gain knowledge about the world around him. Children learn better when they have something visual and concrete to accompany a lesson (Jenson, 2005). This is particularly true of children with autism. When you are reading, stop to ask your child to point out particular pictures in the book or allow him to hold a book's matching soft toy, puppet or any other item which helps him become more engaged in the story and encourages joint attention.

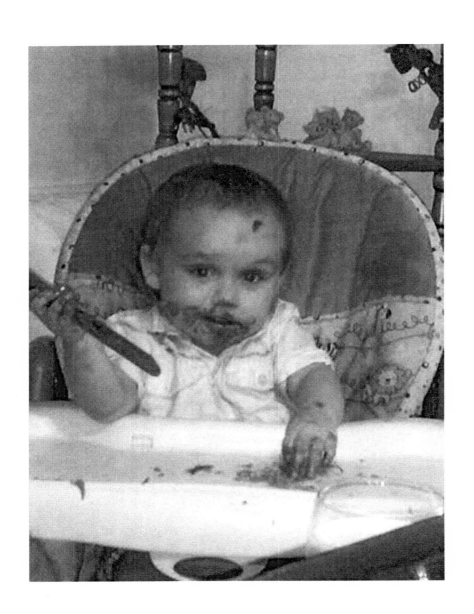

CHAPTER THREE

DSM-5 Autism Diagnosis
Part A: Deficits In Social Interactions

What does it mean to have deficits in social interaction?

Typically, by around seven months of age, infants smile at a familiar face, laugh and express caution when looking at a stranger's face. Through body language, a child learns to understand how another person might be feeling. This type of communication is necessary so that children can share information and emotional feelings with friends and caregivers.

Social interaction is a major developmental goal for all young children. If you were to ask ten different people their definition of important social skills, I believe you would receive ten different answers. Before I left the house to visit a friend, my mother always reminded me, "Don't forget to say please and thank you and have a good time." Certainly a valuable lesson learned. However, social skills and social interaction go well beyond simply having "good manners". Young children's social skills include: how to be part of a group; how to make friends; how to understand and follow rules/ routines; how to express empathy; how to follow directions and how to find ways to help self-regulate their own behaviors. Children learn all of these skills by observing other people, modeling others' behaviors and learning in what educators like to refer to as wonderful "teachable moments."

We spoke earlier about deficits in pragmatic language. In particular, children with autism do not engage in conversation or use other nonverbal ways to share information with other people. With deficits in social communication, it is easy to see why there will also be deficits in social interaction. To be social, we must be able to somehow communicate and share our interests with others.

Social interactions are extremely challenging for children with autism. They use few communicative gestures themselves and they often do not look at people when they are speaking. As a result, they are not observing other people and learning how to understand important modeled behaviors. This also makes it very difficult for them to understand other's social cues. Children with autism need a lot of coaching and instruction on how to learn to read other's feelings and expressions.

My son NEVER looks at me or anyone else when he talks, and often people tell me that is rude. What can I do?

This is a big question, and one that often leads me to my proverbial soap box! Like children with attention deficit disorder, I believe children with autism are over-aware of everything going on around them. There is a misconception that if children are not looking at you, they are not only disrespectful but they are not "paying attention". This is not at all true. In fact, they often are attending to everything going on around them and can become overwhelmed with input from all directions. As for being "rude," this is an area of debate. There are many cultures which frown on a younger person looking at an adult when he speaks; it is seen as a sign of disrespect.

In any case, children with autism often have difficulty with eye gaze. William Stillman, a very successful adult with autism, often speaks about this issue. He explains that if he has to look at a person when he is speaking, he gets so distracted by looking at the speaker's facial features and everything else around him, that he loses track of the conversation. He has vivid memories of people grabbing him by the chin to direct his eyes toward theirs during conversation and he remembers how intrusive it felt to be so directed (Stillman, 2003).

So, don't be disturbed by the lack of eye gaze. Learn to understand that your son is listening. If you want confirmation, you might ask him, "What did you hear me say?" This not only answers the question, "Did you hear me?" but if your son can repeat what he heard, you know he understood (Roberts, 2010).

What can I do to help my child develop appropriate social interaction?

Read books with important social lessons. There are many types of social narratives which emphasize: sharing; how to join in play; taking

turns; waiting; helping out; ways to self-regulate behaviors and recogniz-
ing differences. If your child is struggling in a particular area, ask your
child's teacher or your local children's librarian if she can recommend a
good picture book to read to your child on the topic.

You can write your own social narrative in simple story form for your
child by including pictures of him learning a social skill. Social narratives
can help your child predict others' behaviors in social situations and help
him learn what is expected of him in particular situations (Willis, 2008).
Those of us who teach special education write a lot of social narratives
for our students. If you need some suggestions, ask your child's special
education teacher for some ideas.

Help your child learn to share information and play. Help your
child learn joint attention strategies by following his interest and showing
him your interests. If your child is nonverbal, help him learn to physically
point. Earlier we spoke about putting things out of reach so your child
has to somehow communicate to you what he wants. This is not only a
good strategy to encourage your child to communicate, but it is another
way to share attention.

Peer to peer social interaction. As much as you can, help your child
learn to play with other children—peers and siblings. Since play must be
based on a mutual interest and children with autism rarely initiate play,
you can help by matching your child's interests to those of others who are
more socially assertive and then help them learn to play together.

Help with social cues. Remember, children with autism often have a
difficult time reading social cues. You can facilitate social interaction for
your child by giving him words to express his feelings, and by teaching
him the meaning of non-verbal conversation. When opportunities present themselves, families can share their emotions, while also pointing out
the physical features of the person. For example, "Look, she is so happy!
She is laughing, she has a smile on her face, she is laughing and she's
clapping" (Hoover & Roberts, 2013).

CHAPTER FOUR

DSM-5 Autism Diagnosis
Part B: Restricted, Repetitive Patterns Of Behavior, Interests, Or Activities

For an autism diagnosis, the DSM-5 Part B states that at least two of four areas of restricted, repetitive patterns of behavior, interests, or activities must be demonstrated. The four areas listed are:

a. Stereotypical or repetitive movements;

b. Insistence on sameness;

c. Highly restricted and/or fixative interests;

d. Hypo- or hyper-sensory sensitivity or unusual interests in the sensory aspects of his environment.

What is meant by "restricted, repetitive patterns of behavior, interests, or activities"?

This is complicated. Every person is unique, and our personalities, temperaments and our cultures generally guide our behaviors. However, there are some behavioral traits that are common in children with autism which might set them apart in social interactions. The DSM-5 suggests that to receive a diagnosis of autism, a child must present with at *least two of the following four patterns of behavior.* (So, you shouldn't expect to see every one of these behaviors in every child with autism.) These patterns of behavior include:

(1) Stereotypical or repetitive movements, use of objects or speech.

A child who exhibits these movements might walk back and forth, flap arms at sides, touch something or flip it over, or spin it over and over consistently each day, or engage in other stimulating behaviors. Often the child does not play with objects or toys in the way that they were intended for play. Instead, he may line up objects, spin the wheels of cars, or walk around with toys in his hands without playing at all. This child might also use echolalia—repeating (echoing) others words—instead of engaging in conversation turn-taking. Or he might speak in peculiar phrases which do not relate to any topic or current conversation.

(2) Insistence on sameness.

Children with autism often insist that things stay the same. While every young child benefits from a structured day, many children with autism are *dependent* on a structured day and stringent schedule. When a schedule is changed, the child may be easily upset and have a difficult time adjusting to the change. Children who insist on sameness might only eat particular foods or sit in a particular chair, or may need to move from one place to another exactly the same way each time every day.

(3) Highly restricted, fixated interests that are abnormal in intensity or focus.

Many children with autism are focused on one item or attached to a particular subject—dinosaurs, trains, cars, computer games, etc. They may focus on the item or subject solitarily without any consideration of time or place.

(4) Hyper- or hypo-reactivity to sensory input or unusual interest in sensory aspects of the environment.

Many children with autism are over-sensitive and some are under-sensitive to things in their environment. Professionals often refer to this as "Sensory Processing Disorder"—or SPD. This is one trait which is commonly seen in children with autism.

In the special education classroom, we see this in children who are sensitive to loud noises; who cover their ears whenever a bell rings, or the fire alarm sounds. Children with sensory disorder often complain about the feeling of tags on the inside of their shirts, bumps in their socks, another person's touch, and/or food textures and colors.

Some children do not respond to something that is too hot or too cold. Others may dislike certain textures such as paints, play dough, etc., different smells, and some are fascinated with lights or particular movements in objects. And many children with SPD put things in their mouth or smell everything to further explore the world around them. Often children with hyper or hypo-reactivity benefit from some occupational therapy to help them compensate for the sensory challenges in their environment.

You mention children putting things in their mouths or smelling things to further explore their environment. Isn't that a normal area of development for young children?

Absolutely. It is a very important area of development for very young children—infants and toddlers. However, if mouthing and smelling everything continues beyond those developmental periods, it is not age-appropriate typical development.

My son loves trains and his special education teacher is worried because he does not play with anything else. I don't understand why being interested in a particular subject or object is unusual. Don't most children have such interests?

You're absolutely right. Most children do have specific interests and they share those interests with friends and family members. The key point here is, "they share those interests". And, while they love to share their interest, children with autism do not always understand that not everyone shares the same enthusiasm they have on the topic. The social sharing—and particularly, the give and take of sharing information—is not fully understood.

There is great variability among children with autism and their interests from Level One to Level Three. The difficulty arises when it is time to move onto something else and the child with autism is so completely absorbed in the interest that he is unable to comply. In the preschool special education classroom—as we try to engage young children in a variety of activities to help prepare them for their elementary school years—this is often where we begin to see challenging behaviors. This might be the teacher's concern.

Can you tell me more about sensory processing disorder in autism? I want, particularly, to learn what to look for in my child. He does not talk so he cannot tell me when many things are bothering him.

Of course, I'll do my best to cover a broad topic in a few paragraphs! As I mentioned, sensory processing disorder (SPD) is very common in children with autism. Let me say first that while it is common for children on the autism spectrum to feel things that everyone else feels, it is important that we all understand they often feel things with much more intensity.

Because they feel so intensely, they may have more violent tantrums, cry a lot harder, and sensory issues may be much more pronounced.

When we discuss SPD we must consider all of our senses and sensory systems: touch (sometimes referred to as tactile), smell, hearing, sight, taste, proprioception (our own sense of the space we occupy), and vestibular (our movement and balance). Children with SPD often have one or more specific sense with which they over-react, or under-react when things happen in their environment. Because of their strong perception of the world around them, children with SPD may also have coordination problems.

In addition to over-reacting and under-reacting to senses, it is believed that many children with autism may actually tangle, or mix their senses—or have what is called, "synesthesia" (Norton, 2013). For instance, when they see a particular color, they may also be able to taste the color. Or they may smell something and at the same time hear a specific sound, or see a picture in the smell. It makes sense—doesn't it—that with all of the sensory information and potential mixing of senses, children with autism are often on "sensory overload"?

Please be forever mindful that SPD can be truly painful for your child. You will need to do some homework yourself to learn how and when your son is struggling, and what might have triggered his behavior. Is it a particular time of day? Are you outside, inside? Did you change a routine? Has the season changed, so dressing and outdoor routines have changed? This takes time and patience. Remember, you know your child better than anyone. Please share your information with your son's physicians and his education team.

As a special educator, I see many children with SPD. Some sensory reactions are more common, which make it a bit easier to understand how to lessen sensory sensitivity. On the following chart, I am including some sensory issues I see often in the special education classroom and those I hear about through families of students in my classroom. I've listed the sense, the behaviors that often accompany overstimulation of the sense, and—if you recognize some of the symptoms listed—some strategies you might like to consider to alleviate your son's reactions. Again, I ask you to be mindful that this is a huge topic, and I can touch upon it only briefly.

Possible Sensory Processing Disorder Triggers And Strategies

Sense Involved	Possible Reactions	Potential Cause of Reaction	Strategies Which Might Help
Hearing	Covers ears. Cries. Screams. Runs to find a quiet hiding place. Very uncomfortable sitting in place—figits constantly. Trouble sleeping.	Loud noises—fire alarm, smoke detectors, vacuum cleaners, lawn mowers, etc.. Certain sounds—high/low pitch. Particular voice(s). Sound of fans/or heating units. Noise from fluorescent lighting (noises most people don't notice or hear). Sound of chewing. Things are too quiet, needs more "noise".	Calming music. Quiet place to be by himself. Headphones with or without music to drown out loud or annoying sounds/noises. "White noise" at night—run a fan or air cleaner to hear the constant comforting sound. Play calming music to cover other sounds (or produce sounds if he needs it) to help him get to sleep.
Sight	Covers eyes. Screams. At mealtime may not eat. Won't play with some toys—or always sorts particular toys out of a group. Puts items in line order.	Blinking lights/strobe lights/flickering fluorescent lights. Sun light too bright. Too much stimulation on walls (pictures, etc.) Dislikes particular colors in toys and/or objects so won't play with them. Will eat only particular colors of food. Needs "visual order" so lines up items to play.	Sunglasses or visor for sun. Reduce wall art which is sometimes over-stimulating. Introduce varied color foods a little at a time—try mixing with preferred food colors/textures. Use a lamp light when possible and cover fluorescent lights with filters which block out the flickering. Encourage and teach different ways to play with items appropriately, rather than letting him continue to simply line up items.

Sense Involved	Possible Reactions	Potential Cause of Reaction	Strategies Which Might Help
Smell	Screams. Covers face or plugs nose. Gags. Gets frequent headaches. Repeatedly smells particular items.	Extremely sensitive to particular odors including (not limited to): perfumes, bathrooms, smoke, cooking/baking foods, laundry detergent on clothes and air fresheners. May enjoy specific smells, so repeatedly smells objects (i.e. books, blankets, toys, etc.).	Boil baking spices on the stove (cinnamon, allspice, etc.) instead of using air fresheners. Try calming and/ or no scents for bath time and for sleeping. Refrain from perfumes and deodorants which may be overwhelming. Avoid using chemical cleaners and perfumed laundry detergents.
Taste	Gags. Spits out food. Screams. Mealtime may not eat. Throws up. Refuses to eat. Eats the same thing every day for every meal.	Doesn't like particular colors of food. Doesn't like particular textures of foods. Taste sensitive to particular spices, i.e., salt, sweet, sour, spicy—may like or dislike any of the categories.	Introduce foods a little at a time. Try mixing textures/ taste and color differences with preferred foods. Serve a variety of foods from different food groups to help him maintain a balanced diet (i.e., if he won't drink milk, try cheese or yogurt). Follow up with a physician if eating issues are persistent and worrisome.
Touch	Cries. Refuses to touch. Pulls on or takes clothing and shoes on and off. Refuses to get dressed or put on shoes, etc.	Sensitivity to fabric textures and tags on clothing. Bothered by bumps/seams on socks. Clothing feels too tight.	Cut tags off clothing. Purchase seamless socks and underwear.

Sense Involved	Possible Reactions	Potential Cause of Reaction	Strategies Which Might Help
Touch (*continued*)	Will not participate in activities which involve touching various textures (play dough, etc.)	Doesn't like different textures in items such as play dough, paint, outdoor play equipment, etc.	Introduce textures slowly during play opportunities. Provide brushes, containers for paint and other items for play to expose him to different textures.
Proprioception (Sense of individual space within one's environment.)	Pushing. Hitting. Biting. Bumps into others. May be a bit unco-ordinated. Very uncomfortable sitting and/or standing in place. Temper tantrums in times of transition or out of routines (leaving for school, at the store, etc.) Flapping hands or other stimulating behaviors.	Other people are in too close proximity. Crowded rooms/spaces. Uncomfortable learning how to get into line with a group because he doesn't have a sense of his space. Being touched by another person who he feels is in his space (even though he may be in another person's space.) Feels himself getting upset and loses control because he doesn't know what to do with his body. Changes in daily routine so he doesn't know what to do or when. Nervous system is poorly regulated.	Deep pressure: Rub his hands or squeeze them tightly and/or give him deep hugs when he is upset. Many children with autism need this to help them realize their space. On the other hand, some children do not want to be touched, so they need a quiet place to go when they are upset. Sameness—same seat at the table, same daily routines, time schedules, etc. When there are changes that need to be made, let him know in advance as much as possible. Avoid taking him shopping at a busy time of the day when there might be too many people for his comfort. Try to eliminate demands on the child which may be overwhelming.

Sense Involved	Possible Reactions	Potential Cause of Reaction	Strategies Which Might Help
Vestibular (The inner ear's detection of movement and changes in body movement and balance.)	Won't engage in play that requires a lot of movement and tends to be an observer. -Or- Can't get enough of play with constant movement. Odd gait and difficulty with balance. Difficulty with motor planning. Bumps into things. Likes to spin, jump and roll.	Hyper-sensitivity to a lot of motor movement. -Or- Hypo-sensitivity to a lot of motor movement—craves constant motion.	Provide opportunities to swing, spin, jump and practice balance for children who are both hyper-sensitive and hypo-sensitive.

My daughter flaps her hands about the sides of her body and on both sides of her face. Her teacher said it is "stimming". Why does she do this?

Stimulating behaviors or "stimming" are actually behaviors which help your daughter regulate her nervous system. Just as some of us bite our fingernails, chew gum, twist our hair, or tap our fingers to relax our nervous system, your daughter finds comfort in what we refer to as "hand flapping". Many children with autism engage in stimulating behaviors because they are overwhelmed with their environment and stimming serves to calm them (Vigo, 2014). Others engage in these behaviors because their nervous systems require more stimulation. Some stimulating behaviors are brought on by children with poor social skills who do not know how to appropriately engage socially or how to socially communicate with others.

Just as fingernail biting and other behaviors become habits, so can hand flapping. As your daughter gets older and her nervous system is better developed and easier for her to regulate, the stimulating behaviors should decrease. Additionally, through what professionals term a "shaping process" your daughter's educators can help your daughter develop socially appropriate behaviors that can be gradually substituted for the stimulating behavior.

CHAPTER FIVE

Autism Diagnosis DSM-5
Parts C, D & E

PART C

Symptoms must be present in the early developmental period (even though the person may not show signs until he is older and struggling and/or has had time, as he gets older, to learn strategies to compensate for autism deficits)).

I have twin 3-year old daughters. When I had both girls tested, the developmental specialists diagnosed one with autism and the other with a language delay—no other signs of developmental delays (i.e. autism). The one diagnosed with autism is not yet talking. I understand the other daughter when she speaks, but many people do not. As a result, she is getting services for speech only, while her twin sister is in a preschool special education class at school. The problem is, I believe both have autism. What can I do?

That's a difficult situation. The symptoms must be more prevalent in your daughter with the autism diagnosis since your physician was able to diagnose at an earlier age. Children sometimes do not show signs of autism at an earlier age. The most logical reason this might happen is because the challenges with autism rely heavily on social communication and social play. Children make the transition from solitary play to playing with others between the ages of two and three. When the physician tested your daughter one-to-one, perhaps her social skills were in line with what is expected of a younger child who is still developing socially and emotionally.

If you continue to have concerns, you can wait for a bit and give your daughter six months or so to progress socially and emotionally, and then ask to have her tested/screened again. I believe if she does indeed have autism, the social and emotional challenges might become more obvious by that time. Do your homework. There is a lot of statistical data on twins with autism which suggest that if an identical twin has autism, then the other will be affected about 36-95% of the time. In non-identical twins, if one child has autism, then the other is affected about 0-31% of the time (CDC, 2014). Be mindful, however—as I've mentioned several times previously—you know your children better than anyone!

PART D

Symptoms cause significant impairment in the person's social life, in his occupation, or other important areas of his education and life.

What does part D of the DSM-5—symptoms cause significant impairment in the person's social life, in his occupation, or other important areas of his education and life—mean for my preschool daughter?

Your daughter's "occupation" is—as is every preschool child's—play and eventually school. The autism impairment would be seen in your daughter's social skills and communication when she is observed at home and in the community with family and peers in her daily play.

Part E

Symptom impairments are not explained by intellectual disability (ID) or a global developmental delay. However, autism can occur with ID, so to distinguish between the two, social communication must fall below what would be expected for general developmental level.

I don't understand this. My son also has dual diagnoses of intellectual disability and autism, so when he starts kindergarten will he qualify for autism services?

First of all, no matter where your child is educated, the disability does not drive the services or placement he is offered. The services are based on the supports he needs to be academically successful. Secondly, the autism diagnosis requires that in addition to his ID, your son's social communication

must fall well below what might be expected for his developmental level. As I mentioned earlier, autism often is accompanied by other mental health or developmental disabilities, and intellectual disability is a developmental disability which meets that criteria.

CHAPTER SIX

Autism Therapies & Treatments

When I told my friends that my son has autism, they all had ideas for ways to help him. What therapies should I investigate to cure my son's autism?

Please understand that autism is a neurological disorder for which there is no known "cure". However, as you have likely learned from your friends, there are many therapies which have proved successful in helping children with autism learn to compensate for their challenges.

As we discussed earlier, autism presents itself differently with each individual. It stands to reason then that therapies should be considered just as individually. Just because one therapy works for one child, does not mean it will work for every child. Think about what you want for your child and consider therapies and strategies from that perspective. Don't try to do it all at one time. Autism is a developmental delay, so expect things to be gradual—not a quick fix. Just as you expected your infant child to eventually walk, talk, eat solid food, speak and be toilet trained, you did not expect it to happen all at one time.

The following chart briefly outlines some therapies which professionals often recommend for children with autism. The operative word here is "briefly." Again, consider where you might start. As a special educator, I am aware how daunting this task might be, so I've helped many families navigate the choices. I encourage you, therefore, to talk to your developmental physician and/or special educators as a team to learn how your child might benefit from any one or more of these therapies.

SUPPLEMENTAL THERAPIES FOR AUTISM

(Compiled from texts: Stillman, 2007; Autism Scence Foundation, 2013; Brighttots, 2013.)

Therapy/Treatment	What Is It?	Does My Child Need This?	What Can I Expect?
Speech Therapy	Individualized instruction/therapy with a speech pathologist to assist children in language/speech/communication areas of need. [Note: Younger children benefit by attending a preschool program where they are immersed in a program to help them develop language. This is often the best place to start.]	If your child has a difficult time communicating his wants and needs because he is difficult to understand by others, has speech motor irregularities, or if he uses non-functional communication (i.e., echolalia, or memorized phrases).	This type of therapy requires evaluation by a speech pathologist to learn what your child needs, where he exhibits challenges, and what progress he can make through therapy.
Occupational Therapy (OT)	Occupational therapists (OT) help children who struggle with fine motor ability, (i.e. hand to eye motor coordination, writing, eating with utensils, etc.,) and children who exhibit sensory processing disorder.	If your child struggles or avoids using eating and writing utensils (spoons, forks, pencils, crayons) or has many sensory issues, you might consider OT.	You would start with an evaluation by an occupational therapist to learn specific areas of need for your child, where he exhibits challenges, and what progress he can make through therapy.
Physical Therapy (PT)	Physical therapists (PT) help children who struggle with gross motor skills and some sensory processing disorders—especially proprioception (sense of self in space). PT helps to improve a child's walking, sitting, coordination and balance.	If your child has difficulty running, walking, and/or struggles with general gross body strength, he may benefit from PT. Also, if your child has a difficult time defining space, PT may help in that area.	You would start with an evaluation by a physical therapist to learn specific areas of need for your child, where he exhibits challenges, and what progress he can make through therapy.

Therapy/Treatment	What Is It?	Does My Child Need This?	What Can I Expect?
Medications	There is no medication to cure autism. There is medication to treat the symptoms many children with autism exhibit such as irritability, aggression, self-injurious behavior and depression.	If your child is extremely anxious, or shows signs of any irritability, aggression, self-injurious behavior or depression, you should notify your child's physician and discuss treatment options.	Behavioral symptoms require evaluation by a qualified physician to learn what your child needs, where he exhibits challenges, and what progress he can make through medical treatment options.
Teaching Strategies (See Appendix A for a list and outline of strategies.)	Strategies used in the classroom which are taught and generalized for use at home.	Yes. Every child with autism requires individualized specialized instruction.	An individualized education program (IEP) designed to help increase your child's academic success.

I think my son would benefit from some of these therapies. Are they expensive?

Therapies can be costly, only some of which might be covered by your medical insurance. You would need to discuss options with your insurance carrier to learn what might be covered.

I believe preschool children are getting a great deal of language/speech, gross motor, fine motor, social emotional and academic support simply by being part of any preschool program—public or private. This is a time of developmental growth in all areas for all young children. If your child is enrolled in a public special education program—such as early intervention or preschool—he is getting social skills training and other academic skills training which are developmentally appropriate for his age. These skills are embedded in the general curriculum and his particular areas of need are addressed and monitored through his Individualized Education Program (IEP).

Consider also that play is therapy. Children learn to communicate, take on roles, use fine and gross motor skills and learn ways to regulate their behaviors during play. Give your child every opportunity to develop play skills at home and in the community.

If your child is in a public special education program and requires some therapies to be academically successful, he may be eligible for receiving those therapies at school. Some therapies available through public schools include: speech therapy, occupational therapy and physical therapy. I would suggest that you talk to your child's caseworker or special education teacher to learn how he might qualify and benefit from these services through his current individualized education program (IEP). When your child is entering a school age program consider a conversation with your child's caseworker or special education teacher to discuss his IEP and any future therapeutic needs.

One of my friends has her daughter taking therapeutic horseback riding and she tells me it would be good for my five year old son with autism. You don't mention this on your chart—is it really a therapy? And, if so, what does it benefit?

Yes, I am familiar with therapeutic horseback riding. I did not mention it in the therapies because it is sometimes seen as a recreational therapy. Just as many sports support physical development, and many of the martial arts help children with attention and focus, horseback riding has physical and emotional benefits.

My understanding of horseback riding is that it is a good complementary therapy for many reasons. First, there is often an emotional bond between a rider and his horse. This is good for a child with autism who might have a difficult time making friends and understanding people. This sort of "unconditional love" goes a long way toward helping children self-regulate their behaviors. If the child is also responsible for caring for the horse, this helps him develop some responsibility for its care and well-being. These same benefits are available to any child when he can care for and can make an emotional attachment with an animal or a family pet.

Also, when you ride a horse, you must sit upright and adjust your body to stay on the horse (Lifestrong, 2014). This helps those who have low gross and fine motor control strengthen the muscles necessary to right themselves as the horse shifts.

Additionally, many children with motor challenges also do not cross the midline. For example, if they have something on the table in front of them on their left side, they will pick it up with their left hand. If it is moved to the right side, instead of reaching across, they might drop their left hand, and pick it up with their right hand. Crossing the mid-line is an important function because when we are reaching across our body from left to right or vice versa, we are using both the right and left sides of the brain. In any case, in order to hold the reins and guide the horse, the child needs to learn to develop coordination with the right and left side of his body (Lifestrong, 2014).

So, the benefits of horseback riding are both physical and mental development. Plus, the child is outside and having fun!

I have been reading about therapies and different autism treatments online. There is so much information on diets, vitamins, and other medical procedures. How do I know what to choose for my son?

As I mentioned earlier, there is no medical cure for autism, but there are medications that treat autism and its symptoms. Many children with autism do not handle stress the same way others might handle it. They actually feel things much stronger than you or I might feel things under the same circumstances. As a result, your son might be more prone to mental health issues which can be treated with medication. If that is the case, be sure to speak to your developmental physician as he might be able to suggest a medication to help alleviate your son's mood levels and fluctuations which are often associated with autism.

You are right. There is a lot of information to be found on autism. I often feel that all of the information we can receive so immediately is as much a curse as it is a blessing. There are theories about vitamins, dietary intervention and nutrition; therapies which remove metal toxins from the body (chelation); food allergies/sensitivities; auditory integration training; music therapy; neurofeedback, and many more.

Therefore, I advise you to be cautious. Listen to your developmental physician and other professionals who know your child. Autism is a developmental delay—which means your child will be slower to develop. There is no cure, though there are many (who seek only to benefit themselves) who would like the autism community to think otherwise. This is your child—autism does not define him. He simply has autism.

Everyone tells me my son needs ABA. What is ABA?

Behavior analysis is the scientific study of behavior. Studies of behavior help us to understand how we learn and what motivates us to behave one way or the other. Applied Behavior Analysis (ABA) involves the application of behavior analysis principles. The ABA professional works with your child to

learn what behavior patterns can be changed to help him learn and progress socially. ABA approaches to modeling behavior have often been very helpful to persons on the autism spectrum. For example, the professional adopting ABA for your son would work on behaviors which interfere with his learning, including (but not limited to): increasing on-task behaviors so that he is able to work on a task long enough to learn from it; teaching him new skills; helping him maintain appropriate behaviors; helping him learn to generalize behaviors; and helping him decrease his interfering behaviors (CARD, 2014).

ABA often helps a child learn how to make correct choices while providing positive reinforcement for appropriate behavior and educational responses. If you would like to learn more about ABA, you can check out the Center for Autism and Related Disabilities (CARD) and/or Autism Speaks. Their contact information is in the resource section at the end of this book.

Chapter SEVEN
Guidance

My son has temper tantrums which are often out of control. His teachers send home notes nearly every day about his misbehavior. I worry because I don't know why he is so angry, and I can't help him. Are temper tantrums always a part of autism?

No. Temper tantrums are not a part of the autism diagnosis. As I mentioned earlier, children with autism may feel things more intensely and react more strongly than their peers, but it is not an autism trait. Your son is having tantrums because he wants something (often, simply attention), is trying to avoid something or, as is typical with many children with autism, he has some sensory processing issues.

This is a difficult situation. I would first advise that you work with the school and your son's medical teams to try to learn what might trigger your son's behaviors and how those behaviors can be addressed. Remember that you ARE part of a team and we all want what is best for you and your family.

In instances where children are having such extreme behavior, I often request that a behavior specialist visit the classroom. If you, the behavior specialist and your son's teachers agree there is reason for concern, it might be suggested to begin a functional behavior analysis (FBA) and then consider moving forward to conduct a behavior intervention plan. This will include observing your son and tracking data which might help everyone better understand if there is a particular time, place, or activity which triggers his negative behaviors. This is important; remember earlier I mentioned that people do not present negative behaviors unless they want something (attention or thing), are trying to avoid something, or, as is typical with many children with autism, they have some sensory processing issues. It is our job to find out what your son wants or is trying to avoid.

I think this is a great idea, but how will the behaviors be addressed? I mean, how will that help my son behave appropriately?

Nothing will happen quickly. However, if your team is able to learn what might trigger an event, they might also be able to find a way to help your child work through the anxiety or fear. For instance, if your child has a temper tantrum every day when it is time to go outside, everyone would focus closely on that time and learn what might be the underlying issue. Perhaps he won't put his jacket on and he knows he cannot go outside without his jacket. Why won't he put his jacket on? Perhaps it is uncomfortable—tags, or he doesn't like the hood, etc. (This would be an example of a SENSORY PROCESSING ISSUE.)

Maybe he does not want to go to the cafeteria for lunch, so begins throwing furniture around at that time every day when he arrives in the cafeteria. Does he sit to eat at home? Does he not like what he brought for lunch? (What does he WANT?) Is it too difficult for him to sit for an extended period, so he avoids it all together? (What is he trying to AVOID?), Is the cafeteria too loud? (Sensory Processing, again). Maybe he's upset because everyone's so busy that he hasn't had much together time (ATTEN-TION SEEKING BEHAVIOR). These are all questions you'd need to consider as you take on a sort of "detective role" to learn the behavior triggers. Once the team learns what is so upsetting to your son, everyone can work together to find solutions to help him learn to self-regulate his own behaviors.

My son is three years old, and everyone tells me that his behaviors are typical of the "terrible twos-threes" and that he will outgrow them even though he has autism. Is this true?

Be cautious. Yes, there is a period of time when younger children begin to—what I like to call—"test their limits". Learning how to use socially appropriate means for meeting one's needs is developed around three years of age. Because children with autism do have developmental delays, their behaviors might reflect an earlier age. Also, you may recall when we discussed "pragmatic language", that children with autism do not always read social cues and will often say and do things which are socially inappropriate. They might also misinterpret something said to them and react inappropriately in their own defense because they don't quite understand another person's intent.

However, if behaviors persist and are prevalent enough to draw concern from family and professionals, then they should be addressed at any age. Have these discussions with your child's caseworker or special educator and his developmental physician.

My son doesn't talk much and when he does, not everyone understands what he is talking about. I think he gets frustrated and that's when he gets angry and loses control. What do you think about this?

I agree, and I applaud you for finding that trigger in your son's behavior. You may recall that one of the DSM-5 autism diagnoses criteria is a deficit in social communication. When we cannot easily communicate our wants and needs we ALL become frustrated, don't we?

Language and communication development is dependent on our social experiences. Early language development is dependent on input from our family and our community. When children play, they are practicing and experimenting with language with their peers. At the same time they are building their vocabulary and learning how things work in their world.

However, most children with autism—especially those with language delays—get caught up in a vicious circle: They don't always understand social communication and social cues, so they may play solitarily. If they tend to play more solitarily, children with autism do not have the opportunities to play and learn social cues and social communication along with their same age peers. If they have not learned an appropriate way to communicate socially they may not understand how to get their wants and needs met appropriately. This is when children with autism may present negative behaviors. Simply misinterpreting another person's words or intentions might set them up to respond inappropriately—verbally or physically.

This is why I feel it is so important to try to get your son involved in activities with same age peers—in a preschool setting (special or general education), social or play groups, etc. Your son needs opportunities to hear and see appropriate social communication, and to be taught ways to generate those communications himself.

A diagram that I like to use to describe this cycle follows (Roberts, 2010).

Children learn about their social world through playing with others. If they continue to play solitarily, children with autism do not have an opportunity to engage in play and learn social cues, or how to engage in social communication with their same age peers.

Children with autism may not always understand social cues and social communication, so they may play more solitarily.

If they have not played with their same age peers to learn ways to engage in social communication or how to read social cues, children with autism may not know how to get their wants and needs met appropriately. As a result, they are more likely to present socially inappropriate behavior.

CYCLE OF INAPPROPRIATE SOCIAL COMMUNICATION

My daughter has a wonderful sense of humor and loves to tease and play tricks on her brother. However, when he teases her, she gets extremely upset, cries and is difficult to soothe. I try to explain to her that he is just teasing her like she teases him, but she thinks he is very mean. Why would she respond like this?

For lack of a better way to phrase it, let me say that children with autism often have "their own agenda". If you think of your daughter in those terms, maybe it will help. You may recall our discussion earlier about deficits in pragmatic language—understanding social cues and social communication. That is where the communication first breaks down. You might also have heard a professional say that children with autism have deficits in theory of mind. This means that they don't understand how their own mind works differently than another person's mind. They assume that everyone thinks the same thing, the same way, and at the same time they are having thoughts. If they adore trains, they assume everyone else adores trains. If they are doing something that they love, they assume everyone else should love doing the same thing. It probably never occurs to your daughter that your son is teasing her. In spite of the fact that she's said something to him teasingly, she probably wasn't in that moment when he said it to her. Does that makes sense?

Something else to keep in mind: children with autism do not always understand sarcasm or abstract language. Because they are often very literal, what you might think is humorous sarcasm the child with autism might find extremely hurtful and might therefore respond negatively.

My son is in child care in special education preschool in the afternoon five days a week. He loves school and often brings his backpack to me when he is not in school. I am a single parent with a job which often means shift changes and I know my son has difficult days when my shift changes. Can you tell me why this might happen and what I can do to help him?

We see that a lot in preschool. All young children need routines, regardless of whether they have autism. They need to know what to expect so that they can make some sense out of their young lives. Remember, the DSM-5 suggests that children with autism especially require "sameness". While you cannot change your shift fluctuations, you can make sure that everything else is as routine as possible.

A great place to start is to make up a schedule for your son's waking time, playing time, drop off and pick up at school time, mealtime and bedtime. Within the schedule, set up routines. For instance, 7:00 a.m. when you get up, you have breakfast, then you brush your teeth, then you get dressed, etc. And, at 7:30 p.m. you take a bath, put on your pajamas, get in bed, we read one story, then lights out by 8:00 p.m.

The thing is, when you set up the schedule, you need to stick to it! You might start by taking pictures of your son in his daily routines so that he can follow them each step, every day. Your son can help take the pictures and put them in routine order. This will give him more incentive to be involved and to learn the routines every day. You could let him change the pictures around when your schedule changes so that he can easily see the changes, and—more importantly—be ready for the changes.

My son is "a runner". I worry about his safety because he is like a little Houdini who can get out of anywhere—and he's fast. I've tried gates and covered door knobs without success to prevent him from opening the door and running outside. Is this common in autism? What can I do to help keep him safe?

Oh yes, we have many runners—or "elopers" as they're often called!

However, this is not just a common trait in autism—we see it across the classroom in young children with varied developmental delays and disabilities. More often than not, in the classroom it becomes a fun chasing game for them as in "Come get me!" I hope you always alert the adults in your son's charge that he is a runner; it's always best to be one step ahead (no pun intended)!

There are some things you can do. You can put locks on the inside of the door that are out of reach—that even with a chair, your son can't reach. Or, try a bell on the inside of your door—like those that ring at a speciality store—one that you can hear as soon as someone comes or goes from the room. You can also use a triangular shape door stop by putting it inside the door to keep it closed, rather than to hold the door open. It is often too difficult for children to get the doorstops out from under the door, nor can they easily open the door when it is in place.

If you are particularly worried about your son leaving your neighborhood and if you are technically savvy, you might consider purchasing a tracking device for families of "at risk individuals". Your local police department or sheriff's office should have more information on programs run by the County or State. There are also some products on the market now which are worn like a wrist watch. The watch transmits an alarm to your smartphone, computer, or a portable receiver when your son wanders from the perimeter you've set. It works the other way too. If your son is lost, he just pushes a button and the device sends an alert and his location (Project Lifesavers, 2014).

Chapter EIGHT
What About The Future?

That's a loaded question! However, I know as I was raising my own son, I often thought down the road rather than day to day. But, as parents of children with autism, we are not alone. I have it from the best authority— friends and siblings who are now parents and grandparents—that there are none among us who don't wonder what life will be like for our children as they grow into adulthood. Sure, it's a bit different with us, because we might have to push a little harder, understand a little better, and advocate more strongly than parents of our children's typical peers. But, when it is all said and done, aren't we better parents than we might otherwise have been?

Admittedly, my son is now an adult with autism, so I have the advantage of looking and thinking a lot in retrospect. However, I do continue to look forward, and I know I always will. I'm just here to tell you that I understand your journey a little better, and I have to admit, I'm a bit envious that I can't do it all again. My advice for your future would be:

Be cautious. There is a lot of information on autism cures, therapies, theories, etc. that might not be in your family's best interest;

Be aware. That there is still so much to learn;

Understand. As a special educator, I feel so privileged to accompany you for just a short time. You have so many resources, and so many people who now understand autism and who want to help you;

Enjoy the journey, lessons and blessings that are given to you through your child with autism. And together, let's continue to talk about autism in early childhood as educators and parents.

Appendix A

Strategies In Teaching Students With Autism Spectrum Disorder (ASD)

If your child attends public school and is enrolled in a special education program, you will meet with your child's teacher and other professionals at the school to develop your child's Individualized Education Program (IEP). As an important member of the IEP team, you will meet to discuss and to determine what services your child might need to be academically successful. Those of us who have been in special education tend to have our own "jargon" and we often need a bit of prompting to remind us that the terminology is not as understandable to someone new to the process!

The following chart outlines a few of the classroom strategies you may recognize throughout your child's education.

STRATEGIES IN TEACHING STUDENTS WITH AUTISM SPECTRUM DISORDER (ASD}		
STRATEGY	AGE	KEY FEATURES
Social Skills Instruction	K+	(Reading and listening to social narratives relative to the child's social skills.) **Seek to answer "WH" questions** (Learning to answer "who, what, where, when" questions is an important early language development skill. Answering "WH" questions requires more than a "yes" or "no" response and helps the child learn how to participate in the back and forth of conversation while collecting more information about the world in which they live.) **Improve perspective taking** (It is often difficult for a child with autism to understand how another person is feeling and what another person might be thinking in different circumstances.) **Highlights important social cues** (Children with autism do not always understand body language or different facial emotions. They often need to learn to read such social cues through direct teaching rather than noticing and copying another child's behaviors.) **Provides examples of appropriate responses** (The give and take of social communication, which includes consideration for the listener's interest, is often an area of need.)
Structured Work Systems	All Ages	**Predictability, visual schedule** **Reinforcement** (Constant recognition of accomplishments.) **Scaffolding** (Taking the child one step further than his last to keep a constant forward progression.) **Arrangement of classroom** (To consider sensory-related areas of need.)

STRATEGY	AGE	KEY FEATURES
Video Modeling	K+	**Visual** Does not require face to face interactions **Targeted skill** Can be self modeling (Many children with autism are very visual learners and can be the "star" of their video to show more appropriate behavioral choices.)
Reinforcement	PS+	**Positive reinforcement** **Individual for student** **Portable, easy to use** **Use with other strategies** (Token economy is a behavior modification technique. The therapists reinforces positive behavior by giving the child something he wants upon completion of a less preferred activity. For instance, when he loves to play with a particular toy, he is first asked to do a less preferred activity in exchange for a turn to play with the toy.)
Positive Behavior Interventions and Supports (PBIS)	All	**Reinforcement** **Individualized for student**
Visual Supports	All	**Examples:** graphic organizer, PECS, videos and pictures **Communication** **Prompting** **Alternative learning styles** **Flash cards** **Technology/computer**
Naturalistic Interventions	PS	**Takes place in the child's natural, day-to-day environment** **Good for generalization** (Creates opportunities to use skills taught with direct instruction in other settings.) **"Not where but how"** (This form of teaching can be done in many settings beyond a classroom.) **Reinforces positive behavior**

STRATEGY	AGE	KEY FEATURES
Naturalistic Interventions (cont'd)	PS	Can create teaching opportunities Flash cards "Home visits" for preschool children
Self Management	3+	Student is responsible for checking Self-contained Self data recording Graphic Clear criteria Reinforcement for meeting criteria Timers Teacher checks data
Peer-Mediated Intervention	PS +	Child centered, peer connections Typically developed students are trained as "peer models" Good for social skills and social narratives Good for generalization away from teacher Play skills Modeling and imitation Predictability
Prompting	All	Gestures Modeling Physical Visual (Different ways of helping to give learners assistance with a specific skill.)

Sources: Heidi J. Graff, Ph.D. 2014; National Professional Development Center (2014). *Wong, C., Odom, S. L., Hume, K. Cox, A. W., Fettig, A., Kucharczyk, S. Brock, M. Plavnick, J., Fleury, V., & Schultz, T. R. (2013). Evidence-based practices for children, youth, and young adults with Autism Spectrum Disorder. Chapel Hill: The University of North Carolina, Frank Porter Graham Child Development Institute, Autism Evidence-Based Practice Review Group.*

References

American Psychiatric Association (2013). *Desk reference to the diagnostic criteria from DSM-5*. Washington, DC: APA.

Autism Science Foundation. (2013). *Treatment options*. Retrieved November 30, 2013 from website: http://www.autismsciencefoiundation.org/what-is-autism-diagnosis/treatment

Autism Society of America. (2014). *Autism and vaccines*. Retrieved April 12, 2014 from http://www.autism-society-org

Autism Society of America. (2014). *Autism causes*. Retrieved April 12, 2014 from website: http://www.autism-society.org/about-autism/causes/

Autism Speaks (2014). Applied Behavior Analysis (ABA). Retrieved July 17, 2014 from website: www.autismspeaks.org

Bright Tots (2013). *Autism therapies*. Retrieved November 30, 2013 from Bright Tots website: http://www.brighttots.com

Bright Tots (2014). *Echolalia in autism*. Retrieved January 22, 2014 from Bright Tots website: http://www.brighttots.com

Bruey, C. (2004). *Demystifying autism spectrum disorders: A guide for parents and professionals*. Bethesda, MD: Woodbine House.

Center for Autism and Related Disabilities (CARD), (2014). *ABA resources: What is ABA?* Retrieved July 17, 2014 from website: www.centerforautism.com/aba-therapy.aspx

Centers for Disease Control. (2014). *10 Things to know about new autism data*. Retrieved March 27, 2014 from website: http://www.cdc.gov

Centers for Disease Control. (2014). *Causes and risk factors*. Retrieved April 12, 2014 from: www.cdc.gov

Hoover, A. & Roberts, K. (2013). *Let's talk about early language development*, Burgess, VA: Fourth Lloyd Productions.

Kluth, P. (2003). *You're going to love this kid! Teaching students with autism in the inclusive classroom*. Baltimore, MD : Paul H. Brookes Publishing.

Lifestrong (2014). *Benefits of horse therapy for kids with autism*. Retrieved January 23, 2014, from website: http://www.livestrong.com/article/85331-benefits-horse-therapy-kids-autism

National Institutes of Health. (2010). *Shared neurobiology of autism and related disorders*. Retrieved February 27, 2010 from www.nih.gov

National Professional Development Center (2014). *Evidence-based practice: Prompting*. Retrieved from Website: http://autismpdc.fpg.unc.edu/content/prompting

Norton, E. (2013). *Autistic people may have a tangling of the senses*. Retrieved November 29, 2013 from Science/AAAS/News website: http://news.sciencemag.org

Project Lifesavers (2013). *At risk tracking device*. Order through website: http://www.projectlifesaver.org/Pal-info

Rao, S. & Gagie, B. (2006). "Learning through seeing and doing: Visual supports for children with autism". *Teaching Exceptional Children*, 38(6), 26-33.

Roberts, K. G. (2010) *Embracing autism: Successful strategies for general education teachers*. Burgess, VA: Fourth Lloyd Productions.

Rutter, M. (2005). "Genetic influences and autism". In F. Volkmar, R. Paul, A. Klin, & D. Cohen (Eds), *Handbook of autism and pervasive development disorders* (pp. 425-452) New York: John Wiley & Sons.

Stillman, W. (2003). *Demystifying the autistic experience: A humanistic introduction for parents, caregivers and educators.* Philadelphia, PA: Jessica Kingsley Publishers.

Vigo, L. (2014). *Why do kids with autism do that?* Retrieved June 22, 2014, from website: http://theautismblog.seattlechildrens.org/why-do-kids-with-autism-do-that

Wong, C., Odom, S. L., Hume, K. Cox, A. W., Fettig, A., Kucharczyk, S. Brock, M. Plavnick, J., Fleury, V., & Schultz, T.R. (2013). *Evidence-based practices for children, youth, and young adults with Autism Spectrum Disorder.* Chapel Hill: The University of North Carolina, Frank Porter Graham Child Development Institute, Autism Evidence-Based Practice Review Group.

Recommended Reading: Author's Favorites:

Bilmes, Jenna, (2012). *Beyond behavior management: The six life skills children need* (2Ed). St. Paul, MN: Redleaf Press.

• A lengthy book, but well worth the read. A wealth of information on understanding children's social and emotional development with strategies to help them when they are struggling with self-control. This book offers many different ways for looking at behavior and better ways for us to express ourselves in order to be one step ahead of negative behaviors in children.

Grandin, T. (1986, 2005). *Emergence. Labeled autistic: A true story.* New York, NY: Warner Books.

Grandin, T. (1995, 2006). *Thinking in pictures: My life with autism.* New York, NY: Vintage Books.

• Temple Grandin is a very successful adult with autism. Her journey from childhood is documented in her books, which are not only inspirational but provide information about autism from her own perspective. These are two of my favorite books. Her life is portrayed in an HBO Movie "Temple Grandin." Dr. Grandin does a lot of public speaking. If you ever have an opportunity to hear her speak, don't pass it up! She's an amazing person.

Hoover, A., Roberts, K. (2013). *Let's talk about early language development.* Burgess, VA: Fourth Lloyd Productions.

• First in the *Let's Talk Series* this book is written for families who have questions about their children's language development. We outline pragmatic language, which is a deficit trait in most children with autism.

Isaacson, R. (2010): Video: *Horse boy: A father's quest to heal his son.* Horse Boy Productions.

• Temple Grandin is interviewed and she discusses how she learned and continues to learn.

Sy, M. (2012). *Temple grandin: How the girl who loved cows embraced autism and changed the world.* New York, NY: Houghton Mifflin.

- Written for parents to read to their young children.

Autism Resources:

The Autism Society of America
4340 East-West Highway, Suite 350
Bethesda, MD 20814
800-328-8476
www.autism.society.org

The ARC National Office
1825 K Street, NW Suite 1200
Washington, DC 20006
800-433-5255
www.thearc.org

Autism Science Foundation
28 West 39th Street, Suite 502
New York, NY 10018
www.autismsciencefoundation.org

Autism Speaks
1 East 33rd Street, 4th Floor
New York, NY 10016
212-252-8584
www.autismspeaks.org

Center for Autism and Related Disabilities (CARD)
Toll free number: 1-855-345-CARD (2273)
www.centerforautism.com

Kenney Krieger Institute
Center for Autism and Related Disorders
3901 Greenspring Avenue
Baltimore, MD 21211
(443) 923-7630.
www.kennedykrieger.org

National Autism Center
www.nationalautismcenter.org/

Autism Internet Modules
www.autisminternetmodules.org/

US Centers for Disease Control & Prevention
Autism Information Center, Washington, DC
http://www.cdc.gov

Karen Griffin Roberts has a Masters in Special Education and a Bachelors of Individualized Study (BIS) in Early Childhood Development: A Study in Autism from George Mason University (GMU). Her GMU undergraduate project to develop a manual for preschool teachers, which provided strategies for including children with autism in the classroom, won George Mason University's BIS award for "Most Creative Project" in May 2009. Worldwide response to the project from preschool administrators, special education and general education preschool teachers and families resulted in the publication of her book, *Embracing Autism in Preschool: Successful Strategies for General Education Teachers* (Fourth Lloyd Productions, 2010).

She is co-author of *Let's Talk About Early Language Development* (2013) which is written in non-technical terms for teachers and parents of young children seeking to understand early language development and to identify atypical development. Hundreds of practical exercises to build language skills for typical, atypical, non-verbal and dual-language children make this book a genuine daily resource and inspiration.

Karen has taught preschool since 1992 and her teaching experience includes work with early childhood learning centers, day care centers and-private preschool programs. In 1998 she was presented with the Children's World Learning Center's Honor Teacher Award and was one of eighteen preschool teachers chosen nationwide to attend the National Association for the Education of Young Children's 1999 Conference in New Orleans. She is currently an early childhood special education teacher for Prince William County Schools, Virginia.

Books by Karen Griffin Roberts

Let's Talk About Early Language Development (2013)

ISBN 978-0-9889391-0-3, 66 pages, $13.50.

Ana Hoover, M.Ed. and Karen Griffin Roberts, M.Ed. help educators and parents of young children to understand language development and how to identify atypical expression. This book contains: hundreds of practical exercises to build skills for typical, atypical, non-verbal and dual-language children; developmental milestones organized in a chart with guidelines to help identify typical and atypical development by age; a developmental chart for speech and sounds; terms defined in layman's language; sections on what language development is; explanations of both expressive and receptive language; explanations of the five areas of language—pragmatics, semantics, morphology, syntax, phonology.

> *Awesome book...will use for book study program with special education staff with plans to develop monthly parent activities. ...parents want their children to do well but do not know simple things they can do to help them. A great resource for this purpose.* —Director, Regional Special Education Program

> *A gold mine of information about developing language and practical suggestions for supporting each child's range of communication skills.* —From the Foreword

Let's Talk About Autism In Early Childhood (2014)

ISBN 978-0-9889391-0-3, 72 pages, $13.75. Karen Griffin Roberts, M.Ed.

Autism! How is such a diagnosis determined for my child? What do I do now? This book helps parents face the challenges of autism with understanding and strength. As the mother of a child with autism and a special education teacher, Karen Roberts demystifies the world of autism explaining in understandable language how such a diagnosis is determined for a child. She answers the questions families have in plain, straight forward language and provides help with real world needs.

> *[This book's approach] is like a raft in the rough sea for those who are struggling with a new diagnosis of one they love and seek clarity in their journey.* —From the Foreword

Embracing Autism In Preschool: Successful Strategies For General Education Teachers (2010)

ISBN 978-0-971-78067-5, 101 pages, $14.95. Karen Griffin Roberts, M.Ed.

This book is for preschool teachers, special educators, speech/language clinicians and parents. Research-based strategies in this book include teacher-tested ideas that support every young child's learning, but especially those on the autism spectrum.

FORTHCOMING 2015
Let's Talk About Early Childhood Social and Emotional Development
by Ana Hoover and Karen G. Roberts

Discounts Available On Quantity Orders!
Contact Nancy Stodart today: stodart@kaballero.com

FOURTH LLOYD PRODUCTIONS, LLC.
512 Old Glebe Point Rd., Burgess, VA 22432   804 453-6394

Titles are available through US, Canadian and European bookstores, Ingram book distributors, and web booksellers including Amazon.com and Amazon.uk.co. Libraries may order from Baker and Taylor.